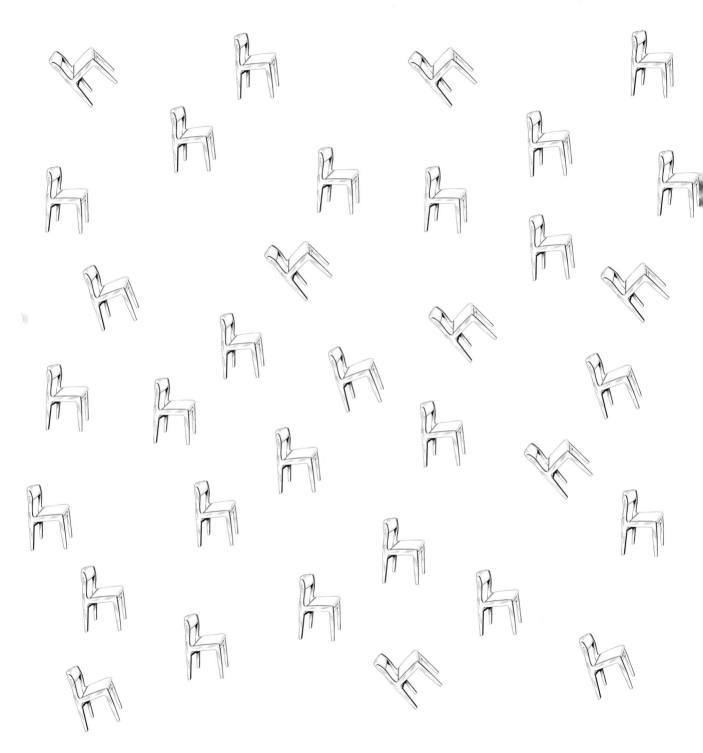

The Children's Place

...At The Heart Of Recovery

Your hooked

The Children's Place

...at the heart of recovery

The Legacy Foundation

The Children's Place

...At The Heart Of Recovery

by Jerry Moe, M.A.

and

Ross Ziegler, M.D.

Published by
Acid Test Productions

Authors: Jerry Moe, M.A. and Ross Ziegler, M.D.
Copy editor: Sherry Sterling
Design: The Printed Page, Punta Gorda, Florida

Acid Test Productions
1370 Industrial Avenue, Suite G
Petaluma, CA 94952
Telephone: 800.983.3352 Website: www.AcidTest.com

Printed in Hong Kong through Acid Test Productions

10 9 8 7 6 5 4 3 2 1

Distributed by Publishers Group West

ISBN# 1-888358-22-X

Please note: The stories and names of the children have been changed to protect their anonymity

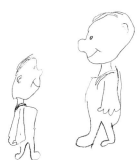

Me Talkin to Jerry

Introduction

by Jerry Moe, M.A.,
Founder of The Children's Place

On a cold, dreary February evening in 1978, one child showed up for the program's first session. Since then, over three thousand children and parents have participated in groups, weekend retreats, and summer camps, all designed to help children initiate and deepen their recovery. The Children's Place has never lost sight of its primary objective—to create a safe place for youngsters to learn, grow, play, and heal.

In the United States alone, there are over eleven million kids living in alcoholic homes. Most silently and eloquently obey the cardinal rule of the addicted family, "don't talk." They are trapped in silence by a family that usually denies the existence of the illness which grips it. These children often have no place to turn, as alcoholism wreaks its own terror, chaos, and pain. Further, they are at high risk to eventually abuse alcohol and other drugs themselves, and thereby perpetuate the disease through their own children.

To break the cycle, children of alcoholics need to learn about addiction in an age-appropriate way, so they can realize that it's not their fault and they are not to blame. They need safe ways to explore and express their anger, fear, hurt, guilt, and shame. They need to know that there are other adults and kids who care about them, safe people who can help. Kids need to learn how to positively cope with the problems at home, such as parental fighting, verbal violence, broken promises, blackouts, and neglect. These children need to learn how to take good care of themselves and stay safe. To escape the world of isolation that has enveloped them they must grieve, be angry, cry, and be comforted.

The good news is that children of alcoholics can and do recover. The Children's Place has helped youngsters develop the insights and skills described above by providing an opportunity for these children to be kids.

Specially designed games and activities help children to play their way to health and understanding. During this process they build upon their strengths, deepen their resilience, and further realize their intrinsic beauty and worth.

This book will help teachers, youth workers, student assistance program facilitators, prevention specialists, and therapists who work with children. It will bring them into the hearts of children living in the entangled world of addiction to alcohol and other drugs. Through their art, letters to addiction, and vignettes about them you can feel the pain, hurt, and anger of these kids, as well as their courage and light—only a glimmer sometimes, but definitely there.

This book is for the kids themselves who can begin to see and feel through the eyes and ears of others that their own experience is real, that it hurts, and that it helps to bring it out into the open in a safe, caring environment.

This book is also for parents. It's been my professional experience over the past 20 years that over 75% of the parents whose children have participated in The Children's Place are also children of alcoholics and addicts themselves. Often the biggest difference between the children and parents is that the latter never had a similar program to go to in their youth. The greatest gift parents can give their children is the gift of their own recovery. The second greatest gift is providing the chance for their children to begin their own healing. Children can't participate in the Children's Place without parental consent. I applaud these parents for giving their children something most of them never got as kids, a safe place to learn, grow, and heal.

What a joy to watch children breaking the family legacy of addiction! They heal as they become reconnected to their hearts. Their drawings and letters depict them in various stages of coming to grips with family addiction. Their courage and strengths shine throughout. There's so much hope! Please join me in celebrating these voices from the heart.

Betsy is ten and full of spunk and mischief. When she started group sessions over a year ago, she was a whiny, angry little girl. With much support, Betsy has opened and allowed others to get close. She's learned to share her feelings, and has begun to gain confidence and love herself. She and her Mom have come a long way, but Betsy still harbors a profound fear—that Mom will relapse. "I'm afraid Mom might start drinking and then things will get bad all over again, maybe worse," she told the group. "What if I can't come here anymore? What if she dies from drinking, what will happen to me?" Others expressed similar concerns. Lucy worries because things are so nice at home that it "can't last." Although his Dad's been clean almost two years, Willie still carefully looks him over when he's late. "Mom drank last week," Brad said painfully, but he was hopeful since "it" had only lasted one day and he was still in group to talk about it. That's the key for these kids. Simply talking—to provide relief from fear, confusion, hurt, and loneliness.

1. **TALK ABOUT YOUR** Feelings, maybe a group.

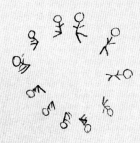

2. Trust people "Maybe a counislor, not everyone is unsafe.

3. Remember all your feelings are ok

Just Remember the feeling may not feel comfortable but all feelings are good even though they may not seem that way.

Oo.I hate this feeling it feels so bad.

9

Group

Sarah spent extra time on her drawing. While usually quite bubbly, she remained quiet and resisted sharing her picture until her best friend, Jaime, playfully coaxed her into showing it. Everyone became silent as they saw a bowling ball and a can of beer flying between Sarah's mom and dad. No one laughed, not even defensively. Sarah described her picture and told how scared she feels when her parents fight.

She wondered out loud, "Why can't I make them stop . . . what is wrong with me?" Others' eyes lit up, and hands shot into the air. Bob talked about the time he had to call the police because his drunk mother was trying to break down the front door. Carlos angrily told how his parents repeatedly get loaded and chase him around the house screaming, "Come here, you dummy!" Sadly, Angela described how she grabs her younger brother and hides under the bed when her parents fight.

One simple, painful picture allowed children to share times of horror, fear, sadness, anger, and shame. These kids saw they were not alone—others knew all too well about parental fighting and drinking.

Donny is a warm, caring, and sensitive twelve year old—the kind of kid you'd like to have. Donny sees clearly that addiction has robbed him of his father. Mention of Dad brings up sadness and tears for him.

"I really need my dad: it's just not the same without him around. No matter what I try it's just not good enough. I can't get his attention. Why won't he listen to me? Why can't I reach him? If only I could get through to him, I know things would be much better."

Donny has tried everything he knows to get love and attention from his dad, and has great difficulty accepting his father's disease. It's hard for Donny not to think something's wrong with him that prevents him from reaching Dad. It fills him with sadness and pain.

She's eleven, and has participated in the Children's Program for over three years. Courageously, Rhonda stands up for herself and sets limits in a way that most adults only wish they could. In many other ways Rhonda takes good care of herself, a cornerstone of recovery for kids. On alternate weekends she visits her actively alcoholic mother. Rhonda deeply loves her mom, yet struggles when mom sneaks drinks during the visits and ends up drunk.

"I can tell when she's been drinking. I pick up the phone, call Dad, and tell him to come pick me up. Mom gets upset with me and swears that she hasn't been drinking. She tries to make me feel guilty about leaving. I ask her to stop doing that!" Rhonda says it's so much easier to pretend everything is fine when it isn't. "I get so sad when I leave early. I love her very much. I really want to be with her," Rhonda shared as tears streamed down her face. "I'm not safe there when she drinks. I end up trying to make her happy by doing everything. I just want to be a kid." Rhonda is learning to do just that—be a kid.

When I was five years old, I thought my dad was the greatest man in the world. I felt safe when he carried me to bed after I'd fallen asleep in the car. I'd half wake up, and go right back to sleep. I loved it when I'd crawl into his lap to read my favorite book before bed.

On Christmas Eve I was so excited about opening the presents under the tree. We waited for Dad to get home; it seemed like forever. When it got close to bedtime, Mom let me open one present, a My Little Pony Play Set.

I heard the adults whispering . . . "How could he do this?" Every few minutes I'd run to the window, because I was sure I'd heard a car, or the garage door. I went to bed and cried myself to sleep. I was sad that I couldn't open my gifts, and scared that maybe Dad was hurt. Most of all, I was confused that Dad never came home on Christmas Eve. My dad was the greatest man in the world. I couldn't believe he would do that to me. My dad loves me.

Erin
(twelve years old)

Kenny, though shy, listened intently in group to understand what was happening at home. As the weeks passed, this eight year old's confidence slowly grew and he spoke of the father he idolized. He painfully told how he rarely spent much time with Dad. As Dad got sicker and sicker, occasionally landing in jail, Kenny repeatedly struggled to win his father's attention. It was hard for Kenny to accept alcohol's incredible power over his dad.

Then, approximately six months into the program, Kenny matter of factly announced that he no longer watched the news with his dad. "Every night for the past couple of years Dad and I split a beer while we

Some consequences lead to JAIL.

watched the news," he told the hushed group. "I really didn't want the beer, I only wanted to be with dad. Last night I told Dad I couldn't watch TV with him anymore because it's not good for a kid to drink beer. I said, 'I hope we can do something else together 'cause I love you.' I kissed Dad on the cheek and left." Startled, the group was silent, and then gave Kenny a loud, spontaneous ovation.

Everyone was awed by Kenny's loving way of caring for himself.

I want to Stop it but I cant

it hurts too much to draw

Janie is a pretty ten year old who scowls most of the time. She's had difficulty making friends and is frequently in trouble at school. She mocked the idea of drawing a picture of her family, yet did it. As she shared her picture, she unleashed a barrage of anger.

"I hate him. He's no father of mine. Look at him! Will you just look at him," she uttered. Startled by Janie's loud booming voice, the other children's eyes all got bigger.

"He sits in that same chair every day, every night until he passes out. Look at his eyes—he's always in a fog. There are his best friends—beer and cigarettes, cigarettes and beer. Why does he have to be my dad. This is not fair. Why me?"

Janie paused, sighed, and stared at the carpet. The group was silent until the co-leader reached for Janie's hand. She quickly embraced him and buried her head in his chest. Slowly, one by one, the other children comforted Janie, a hand on the shoulder, whispered words of encouragement. When group ended, Janie's scowl was gone, at least for a while.

Letters to the Disease

You broke my ♥

♥

I really hate the stupid thing you did
to my dad. If you had'nt done this to
my dad I would still see him alot. His life
wouldnt be all messed up and he wouldnt
have hade to leave us alone.

At the Children's Place, the children participate in an exercise that allows the youngsters to express deep-seated feelings about the disease that has created many of their families' problems. They write letters addressed to "Alcoholism" or "Mr. Addiction." The process helps the children realize their powerlessness over family addiction and co-dependency. It also provides a gateway for kids to initiate their own recovery by taking good care of themselves.

Children quite often express anger, hurt, sadness, fear, guilt, loneliness, and shame. They describe the problems that have overwhelmed their loved ones, as well as their families. The group facilitator may give the youngsters the option of sharing their letters with the group if they so desire. After taking some time to discuss the letters and the feelings that developed as a result of them, the group can symbolically burn or bury these letters to let their feelings go.

Dear Alcoholism,

Why did you take away my dad and mess him up. Why did you make him brake all of those promises that he made, that were so important to me. Why to you make my mom so unhappy with my dad. I hate you so much alcohol. And why do you make my dad want to work all the time and not spend that much time with me.

It is all your falt I want my real dad back,

Leave my dad alone,

I feel up set when I find my dad hiding a beer can.

Dear Alcholism,

right now I'm mad. I'd like to say you killed my Grandpa and help make my family situation worse. Your an addicting drog and it makes me mad your like a fly that goes and buezes around people and won't go away. And people get very annoyed until finally they give in. Then you do your stuff. You pull them into the well deep down in a black hole. Then someone comes along and tries to get them out but won't go in the well. The someome somtimes goes down in to the well and gets them, but only some times. Well goodbye and don't even try to pull me into the well.

Sincerely,
Mr.X
Mr.X

age. 10

Dear Alcoholism, & Drugs

Why did you pick my family? Why won't you let go of my dad? My dad will probably die because of you! He has already lost his drivers license from drunk driving. He can't come to see me unless he is lucky enough to get a ride. I can't live with my mom because of you! I hardly get to see my parents. I can't even call my mom because she can't afford a phone.

I Hate You!

signed
A VERY ANGRY Kid

Dear Mr.
Alclhol

I hat what you've done to my family. As speashuly my Mom because you killed my her. Also I hat what you do to people. I wish you wear never here. I hop some day people mak make a law agenst alclhol!

Dear Alcohalism,
I Don't like what you did to my mom. At least At least my mom is in reavery. You made my mom fall asleep and I would have to feed myself. I was afraid and I was that that she would fall asleep with a cigarette. I don't like it when youl got my parents divorced.

Dear Alcoholism,

you took someone I loved and turned him into hate. He ~~Brock~~ He brock lots of promises. Becaus of you. and he might die because of you. It just is not fair. I cant see him anymore becaus ~~her~~ he drinks. ~~Ever~~ and now I dont even now [if he My Dad] is still alive. I dont like the times and the way he had blackouts. and he hit me, he dindnt now where anything was exepen his Alcohol. he dindnt even now, and I didn't who I was. are my brother and I didn't like the fight that you got him into. You hurt me Dad. leave my Famley alone.

STOP

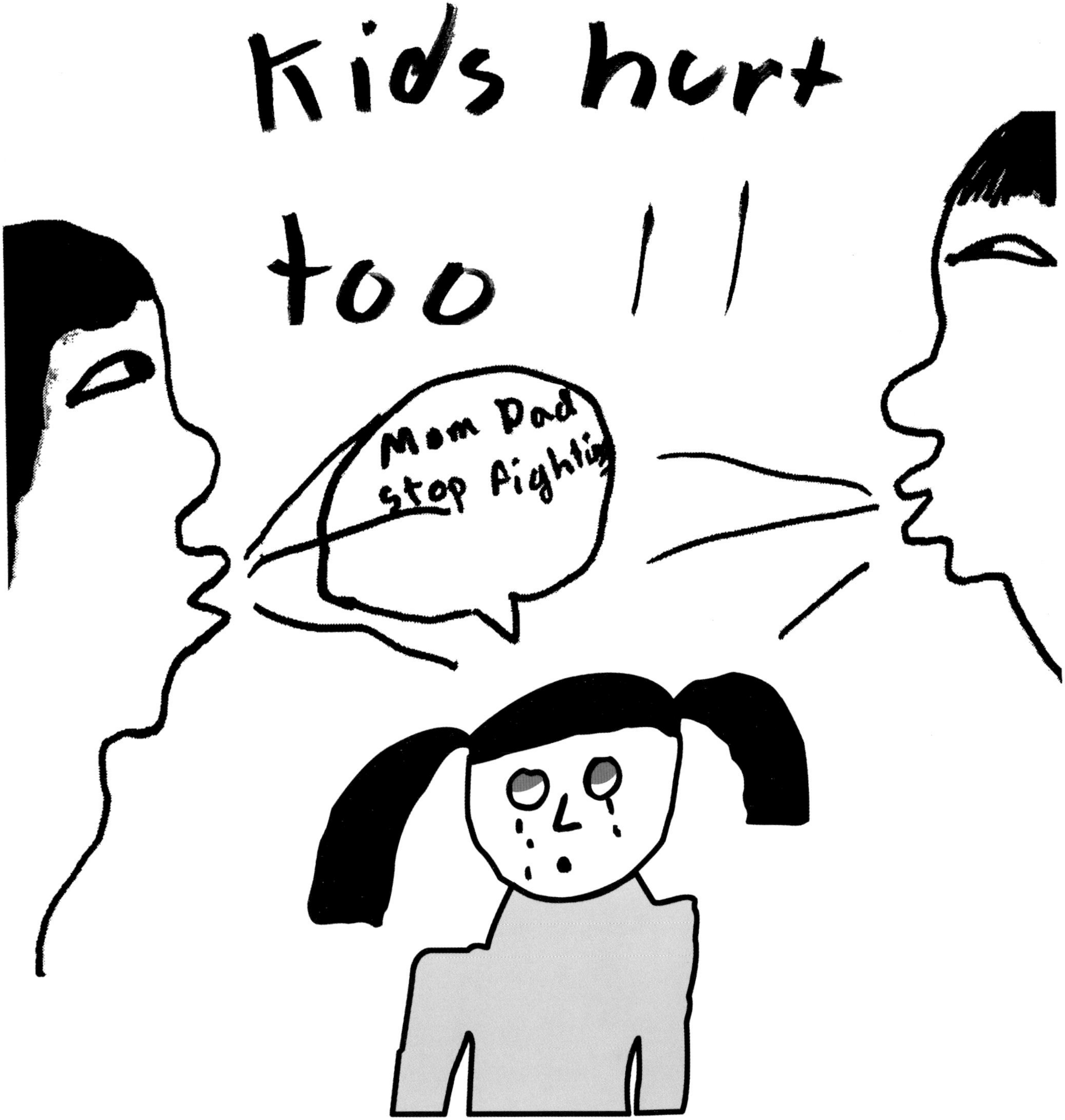
Kids hurt too !!
Mom Dad stop fightin

A Nether brocken
Vase. Just lilke
a heart

When Dad calls (He still drinks

I Was Scared and Afraid When you

Drink

MoM's Not Home

My Mom said
Dad drinks and
Dad said he dont
I am comfused

Dad drinking don't drive me drunk

APICTED TO Beer

DON'T
DRINK
DAD

Dear Alcoholism,

I hate you. Why did you do this to my dad. Why did you make prake the dates. You make kids feel Bad and you stink and Jast Bad!! You Break ~~promise to~~ marrig es, why did you make him take money out of my Bank to drink and take Druggs, Why did you make him for get to pick me Up at soccer. pacter, you sould Get lost and when you do get lost never come Back.

This is when my dad drinks and he ~~askes acks~~ funny O.r when my dad desen't think about me!

This is when my Dad is not drinking! Or when my dad thinks about me!

Dear Alcoholism, age 4

I wish you had never came into my mothers life. You realy hurt my family. Sometimes I think about how you almost distroyed my moms life. My grandma is an aldie too. But she won't admit it. My grandfathers dead so I don't know if he was one too. I hate you!!! So much. I still don't understand why you had to pick my mom. Because she's so special to me. One time when mom had a boyfriend named John they got into a big fight and I got realy scared. I don't know I'm just so afriad and confused I don't know what to do. I'm still scared that my mom is going to have a relaps.

Dear Alcohalism, and my dad is not drinking
iny more. You relly hort my famile
by geting my dad drunk and then
he would yell at ass, my littel
siter is locky my dad stopt
yousin you be for you Kevin
was borne. But I am still mad
at you. I hate you vary
vary vary mouch. I whant
To make you aleagel.
one time my dad touk me
and my siter y to a bar and sead
"I am aly going to get one drink"
but he got 4 of 5 of them.
I hate you

aged

Dear Chemical Dependcy and Drug Addiction

I hate when my dad drinks. My dad does not get violent or anything but he walks funny and acts weird. One time my dad and I went to a baseball game and and we went home he could not even get the key into the car door. My dad thinks I don't know when he drinks but I do. I wish he would stop and get better. Is only you could get people could get better. I go to my meetings and everything, but now they are boring because I not learning anything new. My dad smokes too. Once he tried to stop but didn't I am afraid he might die. My dad makes me do alot of stuff and blames me for things I used to do not things I do now!!! I wish drugs were never invented. I hope someday all drugs and alochol will dissapear forever.

age 11 1/2

Dear Alcoholism,   Your killing children teenagers and adults. I want you out of the world out of all gods creation. God made the world and I don't think he's happy with the way bad people and you treat what he made. I hope I don't run into you. luckly I have my meeting to go to. to learn about Alcohol and Drugs and that one thing you definetly can not ruin.

Your a life threating object. I hate you. You killed my grandfather. He was very special. Now he is gone. luckly my mom got away. from you and is safe. but she is still crazy. I feel sorry for others who can't get away.

Dear Alcoholism,

I am writing you to tell you what I think of you. I really, really hate you. You've taken away a part of my life and childhood. My mother is in recovery. Finally she could control her adiction. I am left permanantly scarred ~~physically~~ emotionally. I really love my mom and I have alway wanted to help her, but I have to deal with my own problems first. Like my mom always says, Let go and Let God.

My step dad has ~~finally~~ adopted me because he really loves me and I love him too. He was also an alcoholic, but he's in recovy ~~the~~ now.

You are the worst enemy I have, and I will fight you for as long as I live. Your death, but I'm life.

The children that can cope
will live on... every one
of us, in our hearts has
hope for a better life, world,
and friendship.
Hand in hand we can cope.

eleven
11 years old

SNEAKING AROUND 4 BEER

I didnt cause,it

and I cant controll it

She drinks aiot of beers

then fall asleep

shes a clean aholic

She doesnt want me to wake her up

Beer

My dad is smoking and drinking drugs

Drugs

trash

Beer cans inside

How I look

My Dad
is in
Bacoury

Me Too

when my mom is on drugs
she is very thin and has rings
under her eyes. It's scary.

When my mom is clean
she is very pretty and
sweet.

I AM happy ~~becouse~~ because my mom
is in recovory

This is me when I'm happy because I can spend a whole day with my dad and he won't drink.

I'm really happy when I come to Kids Kamp!

I'm also happy because I'm getting my braces off in August!

making healthy choices

Seven members of the Children's Program, ranging in age from seven to twelve, were guests on a local, live television talk show. The kids were very excited about the chance to share their recovery as they knew many children would be watching. Initially the show focused only on the crises these youngsters face with parental addiction. It wasn't until the last segment that they were able to communicate their real message of hope. Toward the end, the host asked Doug if he were embarrassed that his friends might see him on television talking about his family's alcoholism. Without hesitation, this ten year old calmly said "No, it's not my fault. I didn't make my Mom alcoholic and it's not my job to make her better. It's not my problem. I'm learning to take care of myself. But I am very proud of her because she is in recovery today."

The other youngsters smiled, and the studio audience gave Doug a rousing ovation.

Such incredible wisdom from a ten year old.

excited

I AM SPECIAL

!I'm happy! I'm me and I don't do drugs!

Celebrating Me!

Though constantly stuck in the middle, between an alcoholic father she rarely saw and a mom who never seemed to have time for her, Doris was confused but courageous. She always tried to please everyone, yet constantly ran away from her feelings. At Kids Kamp, she struggled as lots of those emotions surfaced. She accepted the group's support and was able to grow. When camp ended I found this letter in the staff room.

DORIS' LETTER

My dad is an alcoholic. Camp has taught me a lot. It taught me how to cope with my problems. It helped me to show my feelings. It taught me even though my dad is an alcoholic I will keep loving him. But most of all it taught me that if I am angry or upset at someone and I tell them that, they won't hate me for it. At one meeting we were talking about a problem and I said I was upset. Then you asked if I was mad at you. I told you yes, but you told me to say it like I meant it. I started to cry because I was so scared. But no one laughed at me. A lot of the kids had tears in their eyes. Finely, I said it like I ment it (I did too). But you didn't hate me when I told you I was mad at you. You told me that you loved me. So did everyone else in my meeting. So that's the real important thing I learned in camp. I just want to say that I love everyone here and most of all I love you, Jerry."

P.S. You help me love me.

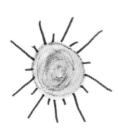

59

Working with young children of alcoholics, we are like itinerant farmers. We plant a lot of seeds, but are rarely around at harvest time. That's the nature of the work. Hopefully, we can give these youngsters tools and skills which will endure long after they've forgotten us.

Last year I received a wedding invitation from Cassie, one of the first kids I ever had in group, over nineteen years ago. Boy, did I feel old! Basically a shy person, I forced myself to go, sure I'd recognize virtually no one. I slipped into a back row of the church just before the wedding march. I was right. I didn't recognize anyone there. In the procession, bridesmaid after bridesmaid went down the aisle. Then the maid of honor passed—it was Tammy from the Children's Program! Although it was twelve years since I had last seen her, I was sure it was Tammy. As she passed, our eyes met and she gave me that same playful wink I had known in group. I simply cried.

Cassie and Tammy first met in the Children's Program. They became very close by helping each other through difficult times of parental drinking and divorce. They maintained that bond and friendship through the years. Tammy was now Cassie's maid of honor! I was deeply moved.

Then Cassie passed—poised, self-confident, beautiful and glowing—a far cry from the little girl who didn't utter a word in sessions during her first month there. Here was the harvest before my eyes. For over twenty years, I've worked with young children of alcoholics in hope of touching their lives. I'm still learning how very deeply they've touched mine.

by Jerry Moe

I feel confident that to say no and don't got with the people drinking and go with my friends.

The Children's Place is supported by the Legacy Foundation, a non-profit 501(C)(3) organization committed to harnessing community resources for prevention, treatment and recovery.

We welcome your inquiries and encourage your contributions. We hope we have stimulated your interest.

The Legacy Foundation
650 Main Street
Redwood City, CA 94063

Could you endow a chair for one child at The Children's Place?

Bibliography

Adger, H., et al. *Children of Alcoholics: Selected Readings*, Ed. S. Abbott. Rockville, MD: NACoA, 1995.

Ackerman, R. J. *Children of Alcoholics: A Guidebook for Educators, Therapists, and Parents*. 2nd ed. Simon & Shuster, 1987.

Al Anon Family Groups. *Alateen: Hope for Children of Alcoholics*. New York: Al Anon Family Groups, 1973.

Black, C. *It Will Never Happen to Me*. Bainbridge Island, WA: M.A.C. Printing, 1981.

Black, C. *My Dad Loves Me. My Dad Has a Disease*. Bainbridge Island, WA: M.A.C. Printing, 1997.

Cork, R. M. *The Forgotten Children*. Toronto: Paperjacks, 1969.

Deutsch, Charles. *Broken Bottles, Broken Dreams: Understanding and Helping Children of Alcoholics*. New York: Teachers College Press, 1982.

Moe, J., C. Brown, and B. LaPorte. *Kids' Power Too: Words to Grow By*. Dallas, TX: Imaginworks, 1996.

Moe, J., Pohlman, D. *Kids' Power: Healing Games for Children of Alcoholics*. Deerfield Beach, FL: Health Communications, 1989.

Moe, J., and P. Ways. *Conducting Support Groups for Elementary Students K/6: A Guide for Educators and Other Professionals*. Minneapolis, MN: Johnson Institute, 1991.

Moe, J. *Discovery…Finding the Buried Treasure: A Prevention/Intervention Program for Youth from High Stress Families*. Tucson, AZ: Stem Publications, 1993.

Wegscheider-Cruse, S. *Another Chance: Hope and Health for the Alcoholic Family*. Palo Alto, CA: Science and Behavior Books, 1981.

Wolin, S., and S. Wolin. *The Resilient Self*. New York: Villard Books, 1993.

Phone Numbers for Youth to Call For Help

Boystown National Hotline .... 1 -800 -448 -3000

CHILDHELP USA Child Abuse hotline 1- 800- 422- 4453

National Youth Crisis Hotline .... 1- 800 -448 -4663

National Association for Children of Alcoholics ..... 1-888- 554 -2627

Note: These calls won't cost you anything because they are toll-free.

You can write to: National Association for Children of Alcoholics, 11426 Rockville Pike, Suite 100, Rockville, Maryland 20852

To get a Kit For Kids that gives accurate information and helpful suggestions for positively coping with family alcoholism check out the website www.health.org/nacoa and click on "Just for Kids" to get the Kit for Kids.

Thank You

We wish to express our heartfelt appreciation to the following people whose donations have made this book possible.

Hap & Lucinda Abbott

David A. Benak

George Borg

Stephanie Brown

Marc & Lyne Cahn

Jerry Callaway

Betsi Carey

Susan Collins & Giulia Rapone

The Dooling Family

Jay, Laura, Casey & Allie Furlong

Emily Garfield

James Guaspari

Cara & Niklas Hallin

Bill Haden

Richard & Emily Hubbert
  in memory of Jennifer

Mary Ann Kaisel

Nicki & Pete Moffat

Phil & Ann Roemer

Ruth & Roy Rogers

Barry Rosen

Mark Smith

Joe Solowiejczk

David & Janice Sonnenberg

Bill & Kelly Waggoner

Mimi Webb

Chuck Williams

Howie Wilcox

Ronald & Ellen Wilcox

Howard Ziegler

Ross Ziegler